W9-BSU-081

CAROL M. HIGHSMITH AND TED LANDPHAIR

VIRGINIA
A PHOTOGRAPHIC TOUR

CRESCENT BOOKS

NEW YORK

PAGE 1: *The National Trust for Historic Preservation restored President James Madison's Montpelier plantation home in Orange County, shown on the cover. Under a templelike structure, Madison dug an ice house. Hawks and owls have alternately built nests inside the hole visible in the temple rim.*

PAGES 2–3: *Three months after the surrender of Fort Sumter, Federal and Confederate forces met on a battlefield for the first time near Bull Run, an obscure creek in Northern Virginia. Contrary to rebel expectations, the humiliating Union defeat hardened President Lincoln's resolve to fight on.*

This 1997 edition is published by Crescent Books, a division of Random House Value Publishing, Inc., 201 East 50th Street, New York, N.Y. 10022.

Crescent Books and colophon are trademarks of Random House Value Publishing, Inc.

Random House New York • Toronto • London • Sydney • Auckland http://www.randomhouse.com/

Printed and bound in China

Library of Congress Cataloging-in-Publication Data
Highsmith, Carol M., 1946–
Virginia / Carol M. Highsmith and Ted Landphair.
p.   cm. — (A photographic tour)
ISBN 0-517-18614-4 (hc: alk. paper)
1. Virginia—Tours. 2. Virginia—Pictorial works.
3. Virginia—Description and travel.
I. Landphair, Ted, 1942– . II. Title. III. Series:
Highsmith, Carol M., 1946–   Photographic tour.
F224.3.H54 1997   97–8027
917.5504´43—dc21   CIP

8 7 6 5 4 3 2 1

Designed by Robert L. Wiser, Archetype Press, Inc., Washington, D.C.

All photographs by Carol M. Highsmith unless otherwise credited: map by XNR Productions, page 5; painting by Peter Rothermel (courtesy of Red Hill, the Patrick Henry National Memorial, Brookneal, Virginia), page 6; Woman's Club of Richmond, page 8; The Jefferson Hotel, Richmond, page 9; The Library of Congress, pages 10, 12, 18–21; Danville Museum of Fine Arts and History, page 11; Mrs. John Fulcher, Hillsville, Virginia, page 13; Roanoke Public Library, Virginia Room, pages 14–15; Mount Vernon Ladies Association, page 16; Tysons Corner Center, page 17

THE AUTHORS GRATEFULLY ACKNOWLEDGE THE SERVICES, ACCOMMODATIONS, AND SUPPORT PROVIDED BY
HILTON HOTELS CORPORATION
AND
THE RICHMOND AIRPORT HILTON
IN CONNECTION WITH THE COMPLETION OF THIS BOOK.

THE AUTHORS ALSO WISH TO THANK THE FOLLOWING FOR THEIR GENEROUS ASSISTANCE AND HOSPITALITY DURING THEIR VISITS TO VIRGINIA:

Jim Babb, Reporter, WWBT-TV, Richmond

Roanoke Valley Convention & Visitors Bureau Catherine Fox, Tourism Development Manager

Metro Richmond Convention & Visitors Bureau Anne Atkinson, Tourism Manager

Colonel Mike Strickler Virginia Military Institute

Lexington Visitors Bureau Jean Tardy Clark, Director of Tourism

Danville Area Chamber of Commerce Debra Dodson, Tourism Director

The Jefferson Hotel, Richmond Ashley Truluck, Director of Public Relations

The Manor at Taylor's Store Lee and Mary Lynn Tucker, Innkeepers

The Page House Inn, Norfolk Stephanie DiBelardino, Innkeeper

The Wedding Cake House, Danville Gloria Newberry, Innkeeper

Sue Bland and Julia Scott Virginia Tourism Corporation

Pamela Jewell, Commonwealth of Virginia Division of Tourism

Jamestown-Yorktown Foundation Deborah Padgett, Media Relations Manager

City of Norfolk Patricia Kelly, Manager of Visitor Marketing

Brian Griggs, Williamsburg Hotel/Motel Association

Ramada Inn Central, Williamsburg

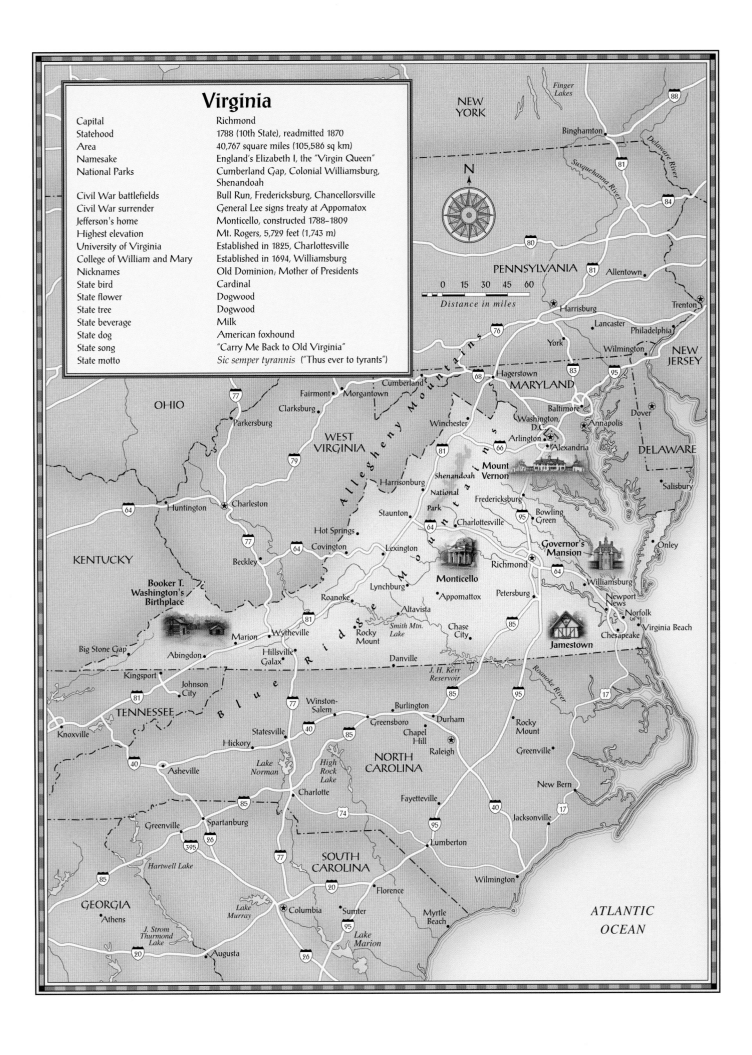

Virginia

Capital	Richmond
Statehood	1788 (10th State), readmitted 1870
Area	40,767 square miles (105,586 sq km)
Namesake	England's Elizabeth I, the "Virgin Queen"
National Parks	Cumberland Gap, Colonial Williamsburg, Shenandoah
Civil War battlefields	Bull Run, Fredericksburg, Chancellorsville
Civil War surrender	General Lee signs treaty at Appomatox
Jefferson's home	Monticello, constructed 1788–1809
Highest elevation	Mt. Rogers, 5,729 feet (1,743 m)
University of Virginia	Established in 1825, Charlottesville
College of William and Mary	Established in 1694, Williamsburg
Nicknames	Old Dominion; Mother of Presidents
State bird	Cardinal
State flower	Dogwood
State tree	Dogwood
State beverage	Milk
State dog	American foxhound
State song	"Carry Me Back to Old Virginia"
State motto	Sic semper tyrannis ("Thus ever to tyrants")

VIRGINIA IS FOR LOVERS, OR SO THE COMMONWEALTH'S slogan goes. History lovers especially. This surprisingly vast domain was named in the early seventeenth century, when all of newly discovered North America that was not Spanish or French was called "Virginia" after Elizabeth, England's "Virgin Queen." It has called itself a commonwealth even into statehood, recalling the time in the 1660s that Charles II of England added the Virginia coat of arms to his shield, joining those of his other dominions, England, Ireland, and Scotland. Thomas Jefferson surveyed much of Virginia and set an "exact description of the limits and boundaries of the state" in 1781. But those borders were inexact out west. Then, as now, the state was bounded on the north by Maryland, east by the Atlantic Ocean, and south by North Carolina. But it stretched far west across the Appalachian Mountains and onward to the Ohio and Mississippi rivers. Thus the early commonwealth was one-third larger than its former motherland's islands of Great Britain and Ireland.

Jefferson's name resounds throughout ancestor-worshiping Virginia to this day. Veteran statehouse observers are pressed to recall the last important political speech in the Old Dominion that did *not* invoke Jefferson's words. And the names and deeds of other legendary Virginians—Pocahontas, Smith, Washington, Madison, Monroe, Wilson (and three other, less-remembered presidents, W. H. Harrison, Tyler, and Taylor), Henry, Randolph, Custis, Lee, Stuart, Jackson, and, more recently, Marshall, Byrd, and Ashe—also have as much currency today as they did generations ago. More than one Virginia visitor has gazed at a nearby thicket through the morning mist and sensed a Rebel column stirring, or tarried on a great white portico and imagined inspiring oratory that sounded some of the first calls for American freedom.

Virginia, however, defies stereotyping. In this single state, one can leave the glistening strand of Virginia Beach for bustling fishing coves, indolent Tidewater marshes, cotton and tobacco fields, apple orchards, plantation homes, reborn colonial villages, explorers' outposts, wayside taverns, giant clothing and cigarette factories, unfettered suburban developments, an array of amazing caverns, the remnants of epic battlefields, and the parallel spines of mountains stretching four hundred miles from Maryland to Tennessee. No one metropolis dominates the state. That's all the better for enjoying the easygoing charms of Richmond, Norfolk, Roanoke, Danville, and other popular locales. Each extols new, vibrant architecture and public art, clubs and amusement parks, convention centers, and sporting venues, while holding tight to a sentimental past.

It is the old that makes Virginia unequaled in America. After all, this is the place that thought of itself as old even in the Civil War, when General George Edward Pickett shouted to his men before leading the last, desperate charge up Cemetery Ridge at the Battle of Gettysburg: "Up, men, and to your posts! Don't forget today that you are from Old Virginia."

How old is "Old Virginny"? Colonization began soon after the dawn of the seventeenth century, on May 13, 1607, when three vessels commissioned by the Virginia Company of London, the *Sarah Constant, Goodspeed,* and *Discovery,* landed at Jamestown and began the first permanent English settlement in the New World. (An earlier colonization attempt at Roanoke Island, in what is now North Carolina, was such a failure that no trace of it or its inhabitants has been found.) The first Virginia colonists named the place in the marshy Tidewater lowlands "James Fort"—later to become Jamestown—after their sovereign, James I, a Scot who was first to call himself King of Great Britain. It was on this spot that more than half of the original 104 struggling colonists would die of malaria, starvation, and wounds suffered in Indian attacks. Here, Pocahontas, daughter of the Indian chief Powhatan, would, according to

Peter Rothermel painted Patrick Henry Before the Virginia House of Burgesses, *which hangs at Red Hill, Henry's last home and burial place in Brookneal in Southside Virginia. He railed against the Stamp Act before the Burgesses at Williamsburg in 1765; his "liberty or death" speech came ten years later in Richmond.*

legend, save Captain John Smith from a violent death. Smith later prospered and even wrote a *Historie of Virginia* that became a prized book on the shelves of Virginia's gentry. In this crude settlement, as nineteenth-century orator Edward Everett would one day proclaim, "the first germs of the mighty republic . . . were planted." The struggling colonists' first fort burned a year after it was built. Its remnants, thought to have been washed away by the shifting currents of the James River, were dramatically uncovered by archaeologists in 1996. In addition to traces of the three-sided fort, the excavators unearthed the skeleton of a man who apparently died of a gunshot wound, and found evidence of glassmaking and copper-working industries, tableware, and blue-glass beads apparently manufactured for trade with the Indians. Looking back, it is little wonder few of the original colonists survived, for several were English gentlemen, accustomed to a life of privilege rather than privation. Though they had been reinforced by two infusions of supplies and recruits, the bedraggled colonists gave up on their enterprise. Fourteen miles into their return to England in 1610, they were met by Lord de la Warre (for whom Delaware would be named) at Mulberry Island, who brought fresh provisions and settlers. The entire party returned to Virginia, this time to stay. Within a decade women and indentured servants had been added to the colony, which began to establish plantations along the James River.

By 1618 the colony had achieved enough stability to convene a House of Burgesses, the first democratically elected legislative body in the New World. A massive Indian attack in 1622, in which more than 350 settlers were killed, ended years of uneasy peace that had begun when Pocahontas married Englishman John Rolfe. Two years later, in a dispute in London over tobacco and other matters, the king revoked the London Company's charter, and Virginia became a royal colony whose borders reached from what is today Pennsylvania to Spanish Florida—and westward as far as land might extend. Not long afterward, Lord Baltimore would be granted a piece of Virginia to form Maryland to the north, while Sir Robert Heath would be given southernmost Virginia as "Carolana." Virginians pressed the Crown for recognition of their House of Burgesses—based in Jamestown—receiving it in 1628. Several times thereafter, the delegates passed "proclamations, ordinances, and orders" that there would be no

In 1900, the Woman's Club of Richmond purchased—then lavishly furnished—an 1858 Italianate villa once belonging to Bolling Walker Haxall, president of the Old Dominion Iron and Nail Works.

taxation without representation. By 1634 the colony had spread sufficiently to create eight "shires," or counties. The colonists even quelled a revolt by residents of the Eastern Shore (the narrow peninsula hanging down from Maryland) who had refused to pay taxes because it had no official status as a shire.

There were then three levels of Virginia society: privileged "cavaliers," or planters—chiefly of tobacco—who held most seats in the House of Burgesses; middle-class "yeomen"; and nonfree laborers, including short-term indentured servants and increasing numbers of black slaves. Gradually, plantations spread westward to the "middle colony" around Williamsburg, and beyond to "frontier land." Except for occasional Indian flare-ups, life was agreeable. In the 1680s, a promotional pamphlet proclaimed that "the land is so rich and so fertile that when a man has fifty acres of ground, two men-servants, a maid and some cattle, neither he nor his wife do anything but visit among their neighbors." In 1693, the colony was prosperous enough to establish a college, William and Mary—named for England's new monarchs—in Williamsburg, which six years later would become the

The Jefferson Hotel's rotunda, shown here in 1907, was a gathering place for Richmond's aristocracy and owner Lewis Ginter's wealthy Yankee friends who were heading farther south for the winter.

new capital. Tobacco dominated the economy of the colony. By 1730, more than twenty million pounds of Virginia tobacco were shipped to England annually. Slaves, just 9 percent of the 70,000 inhabitants in 1700, would comprise 40 percent of a larger population fifty years later as plantation life spread.

Exploration soon extended the colony westward, well past the Blue Ridge Mountains. In 1749, Christopher Gist reached the falls of the Ohio River, near present-day Louisville, Kentucky. Great houses, mills, factories, and libraries appeared. Dutch, French Catholics and Huguenots, English Quakers, Germans, and Irish joined "Virginia gentlemen" in settling these remote lands. According to *Virginia, A Guide to the Old Dominion*, the epic Writers' Project history of Virginia compiled during the Great Depression, "these nonconformists brought a dissent that was to destroy the Anglican establishment and a tough philosophy that was later to override Tidewater and take the lead in revolt against British oppression."

Future revolutionaries, including George Washington, cut their teeth in battle in the Alleghenies during the French and Indian War. In 1767, two years after the Treaty of Paris ended that conflict, frontier lawyer Patrick Henry rose in the House of Burgesses to denounce the British Stamp Act, which taxed the colony without their approval. "If this be treason," he thundered, "make the most of it." A year later, Virginian Richard Bland produced a pamphlet, *An Enquiry into the Rights of the British Colonies*, that declared the colonies to be "no part of the British Empire" but instead independent entities loyal to the Crown. Revolution was in the air; and a committee of legislators, including Richard Henry Lee, Thomas Jefferson, and Patrick Henry, declared itself in sympathy with Massachusetts, which had defied British rule through the Boston Tea Party and other acts of resistance. A "First Virginia Convention" in 1774 elected delegates to a continental congress. It was at a Second Convention a year later in Richmond that Henry stirred the delegates with his cry:

Gentlemen may cry 'Peace! Peace!' but there is no peace. The war is actually begun! . . . Is life so dear or peace so sweet as to be purchased at the price of chains and slavery? Forbid it, Almighty God! I know not what course others may take, but, as for me, give me liberty, or give me death!

Henry's resolution of support for the arming of a militia was adopted. After a Fourth Convention declared that Virginians would protect themselves "against every species of despotism," the colony was declared to be in revolt. Skirmishes were followed by the bombardment of Norfolk by British forces, and Royal Governor Dunmore's ships were driven from the Chesapeake Bay. Having adopted burgess George Mason's "bill of rights" and a revolutionary state constitution that were to become models for other states and a new nation, Virginia colonists sent men and supplies to New England to aid the rebellion. Virginian Richard Henry Lee rose to propose independence in the Continental Congress in Philadelphia, and Thomas Jefferson hastily wrote a Declaration of Independence. It was approved on July 4, 1776, giving birth to a new "United States of America."

Most of the early fighting involving Virginians occurred in the West, at British forts in what is now Illinois and Michigan. The British successfully raided Portsmouth harbor, but an attempted blockade was soon rebuffed. Virginia's key trade lifeline to the West Indies remained unbroken. In 1780, British land forces retook Portsmouth and advanced under the traitorous American general, Benedict Arnold, to Richmond, to where the revolutionary capital had been moved. Washington dispatched his friends, Frenchman Marquis de Lafayette and Prussian

The proprietor of Haden's store in tiny Palmyra, southeast of Charlottesville, made quite an ambitious promise above the entrance in 1912. But could he deliver?

Baron Wilhelm von Steuben, along with thousands of troops, to Virginia. The British pursued Lafayette through south-central Virginia, aiming to take Charlottesville, the rebellious governor Jefferson's hometown, to which the legislature had fled. But Lafayette coaxed the chase back eastward, where the British, now under Lord Charles Cornwallis, settled in at the old colonial "Town of York" in the spring of 1781 to await the British fleet. But a French squadron, blocking the mouth of Chesapeake Bay, prevented the reunion; come fall, a battle-hardened force of patriots and Frenchmen, led by Washington, moved down the peninsula to engage Cornwallis. After a three-week siege, Cornwallis surrendered. On October 19, 1781, the British, to the beat of an apt old tune, "The World Turned Upside Down," marched in defeat from Yorktown to their ships and an ignominious sail home. The new nation's sovereignty was thus confirmed.

Barreling into Danville in 1903, the "Old '97" mail train lost its brakes and plunged off a trestle. Sixteen crewmen died, many of them scalded by steam from the shattered engine.

Virginians took prominent roles in the creation of a national constitution, which Washington's friend, fellow planter James Madison, largely drafted. Washington was elected president of the constitutional convention—and later, in 1789, of the nation itself—and the seven Virginia delegates pressed for the addition of a bill of rights. Virginia was only the tenth new state to ratify the Constitution, however, as arguments over the slavery issue, which the Constitution sidestepped, caused deep divisions within the state convention. Within a year of the peace treaty, Virginia ceded vast territory northwest of the Alleghenies to the United States for future national expansion; and, in 1792, Kentucky broke away from Virginia to become the nation's fifteenth state. Virginia also relinquished title to a far smaller piece of ground—a portion of the one hundred square miles along the Potomac River set aside for a new national capital, Washington, D.C.

Thomas Jefferson was elected president in 1800, to be followed by two trusted friends and fellow Virginians, Madison and James Monroe. Under Jefferson, the nation almost doubled its size with the purchase from France, for $15 million, of the Louisiana Territory, which stretched from the mouth of the Mississippi River to the Canadian border. Expansion continued when Jefferson sent two other Virginians, Meriwether Lewis and William Clark, to explore the West. Madison, as president, paid an unexpected visit to his native state, fleeing the burning of Washington in 1814 during the War of 1812. His successor, Monroe, enunciated principles that became known as the "Monroe Doctrine," announcing U.S. "protection" of the entire Western Hemisphere from further European colonization. By this time, in Monroe's home commonwealth, the University of Virginia had been established at Charlottesville, and slavery was well entrenched on the tobacco and cotton plantations. Twice, measures in the General Assembly that would have freed the state's slaves and authorized African colonization were defeated by slim margins. All the while, emancipation sentiment grew in the state's far-western counties, where few landowners kept slaves.

On October 16, 1859, John Brown and his band of emancipation firebrands seized the federal arsenal at Harper's Ferry, Virginia, only to be captured by marines under Colonel Robert E. Lee. Brown was swiftly tried, convicted of murder and treason, and hanged. At first, Lee—and much of Virginia—felt uncomfortable with talk of leaving the Union. And when South Carolina called for a southern convention to discuss secession, Virginia declined to attend. But

it was a Virginian, Edmund Ruffin, who fired the first shot that led to the capture of Fort Sumter and the beginning of civil war. When President Lincoln called for troops from every state to quell the rebellion, Virginia refused to send its share; two days later the Old Dominion voted to secede. Soon, Richmond was named the capital of the Confederate States of America. Though just 5 percent of Virginians owned slaves—and only 114 of these owned one hundred or more—Virginia had cast its fate with the rest of the region. Lee, already in command of Virginia troops, was named commander-in-chief of Rebel forces.

As the Confederate state nearest to Washington, Virginia became the bloody locus of much of the war, beginning with an embarrassing Union defeat at the first Battle of Bull Run; continuing through fearsome engagements at Petersburg, the Peninsula, Chancellorsville, and the "Wilderness"; and ending with Lee's surrender to Ulysses S. Grant at Appomattox on April 9, 1865. During the fighting, in 1861, antislavery mountain counties peeled away to what was first called the "Restored State of Virginia"—also called "Kanawa"—which two years later became the state of West Virginia. For nearly five years following the surrender, Virginia endured Reconstruction occupation as "Military District No. 1," until the legislature agreed to ratify the Fourteenth and Fifteenth amendments, thereby restoring Virginia to full statehood. Blacks were given a vote, but they and poor whites were effectively disfranchised throughout the South by the imposition of poll taxes. Devastated by war, the Old Dominion's cities grew slowly, and a majority of Virginians remained on plantations and upland farms. The first postwar Virginian to be elected president, Woodrow Wilson of Staunton, was inaugurated in 1913. Thirteen years later, Harry Floyd Byrd was elected the commonwealth's governor, beginning an era of Byrd family domination of state politics.

Inevitable change has altered the face of agrarian Virginia. Suburban sprawl from Washington's Virginia suburbs has spread south to Fredericksburg and the Occoquan River Valley, and westward from Tidewater into James River plantation country, bringing new attitudes and a shift in the political center of gravity, from the "courthouse gang" of central and Southside Virginia to socially progressive—yet still usually fiscally conservative—politicians from the urbanized centers.

Though many downstaters still regard Northern Virginia as a bedroom community of bureaucrats and contractors beholden to the federal government, and think of Tidewater as a transient military preserve—and some urban Virginians, in turn, characterize the vestiges of the old courthouse gang as intractable reactionaries—most Virginians' discourse is remarkably genteel. Some say they still wave the Confederate flag as a symbol of southern pride, heritage, and history—not hatred—but the stars and bars do not appear in the state flag or on public buildings. Tensions ran high in 1996 when someone other than a Confederate hero— and an African American to boot—native Virginian and tennis star Arthur Ashe, was honored with a statue on Richmond's Monument Avenue. Still, it was Virginia, not liberal Massachusetts or Minnesota, that was the first state ever to elect a black governor, Douglas Wilder, the grandson of slaves, in 1989.

It's true that Virginians still speak proudly of "FFVS," a term that everyone from Wachapreague to Winchester understands. An FFV is a First Family of Virginia, an elusive title loosely accorded to old-line families who trace their lineage to early English settlement. And who can blame us, say Virginians, if we revere the great patriots and presidents who were born and declaimed here, or the heroism of our soldiers when more than half of all Civil War battles were fought on our soil? So it is fitting, they say, that the nation's largest naval base, home of the Sixth Fleet, is anchored at Norfolk, and that the honor and gallantry of military service are highly revered. Lacking any major-league teams, we *do* have a major-league sport, Virginians say—politics!—played, here, with uncommon fervor from the remotest county courthouse to the chambers of the General Assembly.

Hillsville pharmacist John Hope built a large playhouse for his children out of thousands of medicine bottles in 1948. Soon a postcard was made of "The House of a Thousand Headaches."

Politics has been all the more fascinating in Virginia because of the clashes of city, rural, and suburban interests. In the Old Dominion, cities like Richmond and Charlottesville and Falls Church are independent and autonomous; they are not part of any county but administer their own schools, police and fire departments, and public services. And they send their own delegations to Richmond. This makes the commonwealth's political stew all the more savory. Ironically, Virginia Republicans, often painted today as old-school conservatives, were once the state's wild-eyed progressives—"Mountain Valley Republicans"—who first bucked the old Byrd family Democratic political machine. It was only when perceived liberals and "laborites" like Wilder and Tidewater's Henry Howell gained prominence that many longtime Democrats deserted the party to become Republicans. Former Democratic governor Mills Godwin of Suffolk, for instance, sat out a term, then ran a second time as a Republican and won, defeating Howell. (Virginia is unique in the nation in forbidding its governors from succeeding themselves. Those who like the idea say this prompts each new governor to work harder and faster to implement an agenda; detractors say the revolving door makes it all too easy to frustrate that agenda and wait until the political game can start all over again.) One result of Virginia's shifting political sands in the late 1900s was the decline in influence of moderate Mountain Valley Republicans, as candidates like Marshall Coleman of Waynesboro were forced to move sharply to the right to win statewide nomination, thus losing both face and elections—in Coleman's case, to Wilder in 1989. Another Mountain Valley Republican, Linwood Holton—elected Virginia's first Republican governor of the twentieth century in 1969—found himself unelectable after declaring in his inaugural address that Virginia should become a model of racial harmony, and sending his daughter to Richmond's public schools.

John Smith came upon what is now the state capital region in 1609, when he sailed up the James and encountered rapids and a pleasant countryside that he named "None-Such." More than a century later, the town that grew there was named Richmond after London's Richmond-on-Thames. Thomas Jefferson designed the domeless state capitol after a Roman temple built in Nîmes, France, in the first century of the Christian era. He and George Washington were on

A maze of trolley tracks had just been laid at downtown Roanoke's main intersection, Campbell Avenue at Jefferson Street, in 1926, and the streets were about to be paved around it.

hand at Saint John's Church in Richmond to hear Patrick Henry's "give me liberty" speech. Edgar Allan Poe was a Richmond native; all manner of southern notables, including James Monroe, J.E.B. Stuart, John Tyler, George Pickett, and Jefferson Davis, are buried at the city's Hollywood Cemetery; and the world's greatest concentration of Rebel memorabilia can be found at the Museum of the Confederacy and the "Confederate White House," the last official residence of Confederate President Jefferson Davis. The city's Monument Avenue began with a lone memorial to Robert E. Lee in an open field outside city limits. But in 1892 the city annexed the area, and the building of a procession of other monuments to Stuart, Davis, Thomas "Stonewall" Jackson, and naval hero Matthew Fontaine Maury began—as did the erection of stately homes along the boulevard. A century later, in 1996, came the addition of the monument to Arthur Ashe.

Richmond is a city of exquisitely groomed neighborhoods, sumptuous estates, more than thirty museums and cultural sites spanning four centuries of history, and extensive decorative cast iron—thanks to the city's many early foundries—said to be a display second only to

New Orleans's ironwork. Richmond is also home to fourteen Fortune 500 companies, with a surprising variety of products produced there. These include Reynolds Wrap, Chapstick lip balm, Marlboro cigarettes, Mrs. Fedarnow's brunswick stew, Oreo and Chips Ahoy! cookies, Virginia Atelier porcelain dolls, Teflon and Mylar compounds, Wonder bread, and Hostess cakes. The "traffic paint" that creates the luminescent lines guiding motorists along highways nationwide is made by Douglas Chemical Company just outside Richmond in Henrico County.

South of Richmond in Central Virginia, the city of Petersburg, which endured the longest military siege in U.S. history during the Civil War, has become a mecca for battlefield buffs. Petersburg marks the northern edge of "Southside" Virginia, a bucolic region long dependent upon tobacco and cotton. Tobacco auctions from mid-August through early November, the most colorful event in the industry, originated in Danville, the region's hub. Chanting at a rate of four hundred words a minute, a good auctioneer can sell at least five hundred lots of tobacco an hour. Thus, a farmer's entire crop, representing a year's labor, can be sold in minutes, after which he or she receives immediate payment. This "Danville system" enables buyers to examine a farmer's entire lot, rather than just a sample, ensuring honest weight and agreeable prices. After the sale, the tobacco is trucked to manufacturing companies' plants, where it is redried, tightly packed in hogsheads, and placed in storage warehouses. After proper aging, it is manufactured into cigarettes and other tobacco products.

Old U.S. Highway 29 winds north from Danville through Lynchburg, Charlottesville, and Warrenton on its way to Arlington, across the Potomac from Washington's Lincoln Memorial. This scenic alternative to the state's interstate highways offers stops at gristmills in Pittsylvania County, the Martinsville auto-racing speedway, the Booker T. Washington National

Farmers line up to unload their modified "prairie schooners" at Roanoke's first market house in 1886. Above the stalls on the second floor was the town's opera house!

George Washington's home, Mount Vernon, looked anything but presidential in 1855. Three years later the Mount Vernon Ladies' Association—the nation's first preservationist organization—bought Washington's home and tomb.

Monument in Franklin County, and the Appomattox Courthouse National Historical Park. Also accessible along this highway are one of the Southeast's last covered bridges in Campbell County, Thomas Jefferson's retreat at Poplar Forest, four accesses to the Blue Ridge Parkway, the University of Virginia and the historic homes of three presidents in and near Charlottesville—Monticello (Jefferson), Montpelier (Madison), and Ash Lawn (Monroe). Vast national cemeteries at Culpepper and Arlington, "Flying Circus" airshows and a gold-mine museum in Fauquier County, and finally, the "Iwo Jima" Marine Corps Memorial—the largest cast-bronze statue in the world, round out the list of attractions to be found. One fascinating stop along the way is Lynchburg, once the locale of a Quaker meetinghouse and now home to the Reverend Jerry Falwell's Thomas Road Baptist Church and Liberty University, the Virginia Episcopal School, the traditional Baptist Virginia Seminary and College, and the nondenominational Randolph-Macon Woman's College.

To the west of this route lie the mountains of Southwest Virginia, and the Shenandoah Valley, which fills a thirty-mile-wide void between the Blue Ridge and Allegheny Mountains. Extreme Southwest Virginia slices so far into the Blue Ridge Highlands that it touches four other states; indeed, Bristol, on the Tennessee border, is closer to three other state capitals than it is to Richmond! Much of the region is coal-mining country, struggling economically, despite tax incentives passed by the General Assembly to keep the industry going. But it is also the beginning of the imposing Cumberland Gap, the first great pass through the mountains to Tennessee, Kentucky, and the West. Daniel Boone led settlers on the Wilderness Trail through this portal in 1775. The region features an 850-foot-long limestone tunnel, Virginia's highest peak (5,729 feet), and a gorge along the Big Sandy River so impressive that it has earned the name

"Grand Canyon of the South." Blacksburg—home to Virginia Tech, the state's "polytechnical institute and state university" and a perennial football power—is a magnet for mountain visitors.

Many modern-day Virginia explorers take a leisurely drive through the mountains via the Blue Ridge Parkway, a 469-mile-long, two-lane scenic roadway. Administered by the National Park Service, the Parkway begins east of Waynesboro and follows the mountain ridge past Roanoke and into North Carolina, where it snakes past Asheville to its terminus in Great Smoky Mountains National Park. In 1996, U.S. Transportation Department Secretary Federico Peña declared the Blue Ridge Parkway one of the nation's first six "All-American Roads."

Delightful Roanoke and its smaller sister city, historic Salem, together call themselves the "Capital of the Blue Ridge." Roanoke, which began as a railroad town called "Big Lick," offers the state's best urban vista—a panoramic view of the entire Roanoke Valley from the Mill Mountain overlook. Nearby are a popular theater, a fine zoo, and the world's largest man-made star—a one-hundred-foot, five-sided specimen. Erected in 1949 and still illuminated at night, it has become the city's symbol. No longer the state's "best-kept secret," Roanoke, a city of 100,000, has been voted among the nation's top thirty metro areas in quality of life, as a place to raise children, in health care, and as a city worth moving to, in separate national studies. Both Roanoke and Salem, the first settlement in the valley, boast thriving farmers' markets. Salem is home to historic houses, tempting antique stores, and Roanoke College, a four-year, private liberal-arts school established in 1842.

Farther up the Shenandoah Valley, small cities like Lexington, Staunton, and Winchester offer a host of allurements. In Lexington, Robert E. Lee spent his last years as president of struggling Washington College. Founded as Augusta Academy and renamed Liberty Hall, the little

Standing amid two megamalls and the cluster of office buildings that surround Northern Virginia's Tyson's Corner today, it is hard to imagine the tranquil scene there a half-century ago.

school was saved from bankruptcy by an endowment of $50,000 in James River Canal Company stock from one of the canal's builders—George Washington, who wrote that the gift was intended "to promote Literature in this rising Empire, and to encourage the Arts, [which] have ever been amongst the warmest wishes of my heart. . . ." Soon thereafter, the institution was renamed again to honor Washington. Thomas J. Jackson, later known as "Stonewall" for his battlefield prowess in the Civil War, married the president's daughter. Lee accepted the presidency in 1865, bringing along his beloved horse, Traveller. In 1883, thirteen years after Lee's death, Stonewall Jackson's only daughter, Julia, unveiled a recumbent marble statue of General Lee, carved by the South's most distinguished sculptor, Edward Valentine of Richmond, in an apse of the college chapel. Lee is buried in a room below—and Traveller outside at the college that, renamed yet again, honored its two greatest figures as Washington and Lee College (now University).

Up the hill in historic Lexington is the Virginia Military Institute, the nation's first state-supported military institute, which opened in 1839. Stonewall Jackson was an early faculty member, as was Matthew Maury. At the Battle of New Market during the Civil War, in 1864, the entire student body engaged Union forces; ten cadets were killed and forty-seven wounded. George C. Marshall, the World War II Army chief of staff who later won a Nobel Peace Prize for his Marshall Plan of economic relief for Europe, was one of many illustrious graduates. In 1996, the institute gave up its long fight to remain a male-only institution and agreed to admit female cadets the following year.

Woodrow Wilson's birthplace, "The Manse" in Staunton, is now a museum of the twenty-eighth president's life and accomplishments. It is a center of refinement, befitting the intellectual president's world leadership. Across town, at the novel Museum of American Frontier Culture, the opposite end of the social spectrum is remembered. This outdoor museum depicts not only a rustic American farm, but also actual English, Ulster, and German farms disassembled in their homelands, moved to the Shenandoah Valley, and rebuilt for interpretation. The four farms create a living history of life in Europe and frontier America during the seventeenth through nineteenth centuries. Incidentally, no one in Staunton seems to have come up with the definitive explanation for the idiosyncratic "Stanton" pronunciation of the city's name.

In 1932, masons march up Shooter's Hill in Alexandria to the dedication of the George Washington Masonic National Memorial, modeled after the lighthouse in Alexandria, Egypt. Washington was the "Worshipful Master" of Masonic Lodge 22.

Country-music star Patsy Cline was born in Winchester at the northern end of the Valley. So was polar explorer Richard Byrd. George Washington kept an office there when he served as aide-de-camp to General Edward Braddock during the French and Indian War. And Winchester was Stonewall Jackson's headquarters during the winter of 1861–62. But, owing to the abundant nearby orchards, the town is best known as the site of the annual Shenandoah Apple Blossom Festival, with its bands, princesses, and fall-foliage celebrations. Just to the east and south, on the way to Washington, D.C., is Virginia's horse and wine country, as well as a procession of luxurious country estates with fashionable Middleburg at its core.

The transition to crowded Northern Virginia is abrupt along Interstate 66, heading east toward Washington. Rolling fields give way to subdivisions, shopping malls, office complexes, the Washington subway's Orange Line stations, and rush-hour traffic gridlock. Nearby

is Dulles International Airport. Once a little-used alternative to Washington's National Airport (also in Virginia, just across the Potomac), it is now a congested hub for overseas flights.

Traffic congestion and the need for more and better roads are obsessions in Northern Virginia and among its delegation to Richmond. The problem, once focused on bottlenecks at bridges over the Potomac River leading to and from the nation's capital, has been compounded by a more recent phenomenon: intra-county and "'round the Beltway" traffic. As high-tech job sites and shopping corridors developed along Interstate 270 in suburban Maryland and I-95 and I-66 in Virginia, and as more and more "telecommuters" began to spend at least parts of their days at home in places like the planned community of Reston, traffic in all directions at several times of day became a challenge. One reason, according to the *Washington Post,* is that Virginia, already home to many white-collar industries feeding the giant federal and state government on contract, is set, at the turn of the twenty-first century, to become a "silicon dominion"—an increasingly thriving center of the computer chipmaking industry—as well. The increasing prosperity of the Northern Virginia workforce presents challenges to officials in counties like Fairfax and Loudoun and Fauquier, and cities like Alexandria, Manassas, and Fredericksburg: how to hold on to open space, racial and occupational diversity, and quaintness in the face of inexorable demands for new government services, office and factory space, and land for subdivisions?

It's a problem familiar to the Tidewater area as well, as independent, rival cities struggle to handle the proliferation of traffic and strip malls that has come with growth. A pleasant problem there, though, is the ever-mounting interest in the area's many museums and historic attractions. These include: the Virginia Air and Space Center in Hampton, a seaport city that was the birthplace of NASA and the original training site for America's first astronauts—the

Sailors were in evidence in downtown Norfolk in 1915. Tidewater Virginia has since grown in numbers of military personnel of all branches, and its shipyards and bases undergird the area economy.

"Mercury Seven"; the Mariners' Museum, an astonishing collection of seafaring instruments, carvings, paintings, and models in Newport News; the U.S. Army Transportation Museum, "where you'll find a truck that walks and a ship that flies," in Fort Eustis; the Chrysler Museum of Art, one of the nation's premier collections of art, photography, and the decorative arts, in downtown Norfolk; and Nauticus, a hands-on naval museum in which visitors learn the skills of ship design, navigation, and exploration, on the Norfolk waterfront. Even one family store is a tourist attraction: Doumar's Drive-In in Norfolk. It was the family's ancestor, Abe Doumar, a Syrian immigrant, who invented the ice-cream cone in 1904 when he borrowed a neighboring vendor's waffle to make a wrapper for his ice cream at the Saint Louis World's Fair.

Tidewater Virginia also has one other charm that no other region of the commonwealth can match: a booming beach community, Virginia Beach, which begins at the 1791 Cape Henry Lighthouse, the spot where John Smith and his fellow pioneers first landed on their way to Jamestown. Where it once encompassed about 1,600 acres, Virginia Beach today covers 310 square miles (many of them well inland), becoming, at better than 400,000, the state's most populous city, replete with concert halls, dance and music clubs, and even an opera house, in addition to its boardwalk rides and other beachfront diversions. Virginia Beach also offers the state's most popular museum—the Virginia Marine Science Museum—which features an aquarium, a Coastal River Room where birds and turtles roam free, a re-created shipwreck, and a six-story IMAX theater complex. In town, as well, is the Life-Saving Museum of Virginia, where the history of real shipwrecks can be studied in detail.

Urban commotion is not a concern along the overlooked finger of land across the 17.6-mile Chesapeake Bay Bridge-Tunnel. It's Virginia's Eastern Shore, the seventy-mile-long "va" portion of the Delmarva (Delaware-Maryland-Virginia) Peninsula. "Heaven and earth never agreed better to frame a place for man's habitation," wrote John Smith after a visit there in 1608. So it is today, insist residents of the peninsula's fishing villages and nearby islands. For more than three centuries until the bay bridge-tunnel was completed in 1964, the Shore was entirely separated by water from its home state. Chincoteague Island, just offshore, includes a national wildlife refuge. And Assateague Island, shared with Maryland, is a protected national seashore. Wild ponies, descended from horses that swam to safety after a Spanish galleon sank, live on Assateague. Once a year, some of them swim over to Chincoteague, where they are penned and sold at auction.

Crowds are very much in vogue, however, at the state's most popular historic attractions—Colonial Williamsburg, Jamestown, and Yorktown. For seventy-seven years, leading to the Declaration of Independence, Williamsburg was the capital of England's oldest, largest, richest, and most populous American colony. Colonial Williamsburg is a reconstituted colonial village covering 173 acres of the original 220-acre town. The village contains eighty-eight original structures, fifty reconstructions (including the original colonial capitol), and forty exhibition buildings. The restoration dates to 1926, when John D. Rockefeller Jr. authorized the purchase of the first restored home.

Two sites mark England's first permanent colony in the New World: Jamestown Colonial

Williamsburg in 1928 (above) was about to get a facelift unprecedented in American history. A nonprofit foundation, Colonial Williamsburg, established that year, would restore and re-create the former colonial capital. George Washington once surveyed the Great Dismal Swamp, straddling the North Carolina border, (shown, opposite, in 1906), seeking a route for a canal between the Chesapeake Bay and Albemarle Sound.

National Historical Park, a National Park Service site, is a five-mile-long exhibit of Jamestown's early life. And Jamestown Settlement, a museum operated by the Commonwealth's Jamestown-Yorktown Foundation, combines indoor and outdoor exhibits, including a re-created Indian village and full-size replicas of the settlers' original ships. Yorktown also boasts a National Park Service site—the historic battlefield and earthworks—as well as the foundation's facility, Yorktown Victory Center, where costumed interpreters depict a Continental Army encampment and a late-eighteenth-century farmsite.

The Historic Triangle also features a decidedly modern attraction—the giant Busch Gardens Williamsburg theme park. An hour away, north of Richmond, another complex of rides and children's amusements, Paramount's King's Dominion, draws customers on Interstate 95.

History is served along old State Route 5, which hugs the James River. There, in a jurisdiction with the odd name "Charles City County," are nine historic plantation homes, some dating to the seventeenth century. These include: Shirley Plantation, the oldest in Virginia, settled in 1613; Berkeley Plantation, site of the first official Thanksgiving in 1619 and the birthplace of President William Henry Harrison; and Sherwood Forest Plantation, home of John Tyler after he served as president.

In the early 1980s, Virginia briefly replaced its widely imitated "Virginia Is for Lovers" slogan in favor of an insipid "These Are Exciting Times in Virginia" campaign. They were indeed exciting times of growth and change, but the commonwealth soon returned to its "lovers" theme. After all, who could argue that the Old Dominion was indeed a place for lovers of languid beaches, tranquil valleys, majestic mountains, antebellum and Victorian architecture, and, above all, history and patriotic tradition?

OVERLEAF: Virginia's restful Eastern Shore— a collection of barrier islands and a piece of a peninsula that includes parts of Delaware and Maryland—is a sailor's and sportsman's Eden. There, America's oldest continuous court records, in Eastville—also site of an old debtors' prison—date to 1632. More than 260 species of birds, and the famous Chincoteague wild ponies, inhabit Assateague Island's wildlife refuge.

Virginia Beach has grown into a sprawling seaside resort—the largest city in the state—but there are still plenty of remote paths and dunes (above). On Cape Henry, Jamestown colonists first touched the shore of the New World in 1607, thirteen years before the Pilgrims landed on Plymouth Rock. Nearby (right), at the point where the Chesapeake Bay spills into the Atlantic Ocean, stand the old, brick Cape Henry Lighthouse, built in 1791—the oldest government-built lighthouse in America and the city's official symbol today—and a newer lighthouse, built in 1879, that still guides ships along the coast. It was off Cape Henry that the French fleet, commanded by Admiral Count de Grasse, stopped the British Fleet during the American Revolution.

Todd Lindbergh was painting billboards in 1987 when the owner of an auto-repair shop asked him to create something unusual on the side of his building. He drew an oversized spark plug. Since then, he and his brother Eric—both high-school dropouts with no artistic training—have painted dozens of murals in the Virginia Beach area, including this underwater scene (left) on a wall of the Sunsations T-shirt shop on Atlantic Avenue. They sign their work "Talent," shorthand for "Todd Alan Lindbergh Enterprises." Up Atlantic Avenue at Thirty-first Street are eminently climbable beach balls—one of the city's many beach-theme public-art displays (above).

The Douglas MacArthur Memorial (opposite) in downtown Norfolk is housed in the city's nineteenth-century City Hall, whose consulting architect, Thomas Walter, designed the dome and two wings of the U.S. Capitol. The general's final resting place in the memorial's rotunda is surrounded by galleries portraying his life. Once elegant, then a slum, now lively and stylish again, the Ghent neighborhood (left) was Norfolk's first planned community. It was named in honor of the signing of the Treaty of Ghent in Belgium that ended the War of 1812 and reopened Norfolk's blockaded harbor. The soaring Freemason Street Baptist Church (above) was built in 1848.

Anna Hyatt Huntington created The Torchbearers *statue (above) outside the Chrysler Museum of Art. The Italianate building displays an encyclopedic collection of more than thirty* thousand objects spanning almost four thousand years of art history. Founded in 1933 as the Norfolk Museum of Arts and Sciences, the museum was renamed in 1971 upon donation of Walter P. Chrysler Jr.'s extensive art collection. The museum also owns and offers tours of three Tidewater historic houses. Norfolk's Wells Theatre (opposite) opened in 1913 as one of the Wells Brothers' group of legitimate theaters, stretching from Evansville, Indiana, to Jacksonville, Florida. Later a burlesque house, "B" movie theater, tacky home to X-rated flicks, and even a gin joint, the theater was saved by the city, beautifully restored with heavy corporate underwriting in late 1980s, and reopened as the home of the Virginia Stage Company.

Nolfolk's waterfront is replete with attractions, including Nauticus, the hands-on National Maritime Center; the Waterside Festival Marketplace; and the U.S. Naval Base (opposite), the largest naval installation in the world. "Pavilions" were originally meeting places of desert travelers and Byzantine traders. At Virginia Beach's Pavilion—its convention center (left)—groups of several hundred or several thousand convene, display products, and attend performances. To the northwest in Hampton Roads, the Hampton Coliseum (above) is the site of an annual jazz festival that has featured many star performers. Here, the term "roads" refers not to a series of highways, but to a shipping channel at the mouth of five rivers, including the James and the Elizabeth.

The Mariners' Museum in Newport News was founded by philanthropist Archer Huntington, son of the owner of the world's largest privately owned shipyard nearby. The museum's collection, exploring the culture of the sea, includes ships' figureheads and murals (above). This figure was placed aboard the Italian bark Saint Michael in 1909. It was removed twenty-four years after the ship ran aground on a coral reef in Jamaica in 1912. Thomas Skinner executed The Foundry mural on canvas in the early 1930s. The museum's elaborate, sculpted bronze front doors (opposite) celebrate the history of shipping and the mythology of the sea. They were designed by Herbert Adams in 1935. There are several stories of how "Newport News" got its name. Newport was a ship's captain and storekeeper who spread "news" both upon docking and through his store.

At Jamestown Settlement, where America's colonial history began, three tall-masted ships—replicas of the three English ships that sailed to Virginia in 1607—lie at anchor in the James River. Aboard one, the Susan Constant (opposite), costumed interpreters guide visitors through the intricacies of seventeenth-century shipboard life. A reconstructed primitive church (above) is one of several buildings inside James Fort at the settlement. In the woods beyond the fort is a Powhatan Indian village, constructed from firsthand descriptions from English settlers. The settlement also offers indoor galleries, in which original artifacts and other exhibits covering the colonists' first hundred years are displayed. Jamestown Settlement and the Yorktown Victory Center at nearby Yorktown— both within twenty minutes of Colonial Williamsburg in Virginia's Historic Triangle—are operated by a foundation that is an educational arm of the Commonwealth of Virginia.

Statues of Pocahantas (above) and Captain John Smith (opposite) can be found at Jamestown Island, part of the National Park Service's Colonial National Historical Park. Pocahantas, the daughter of a chief of thirty coastal tribes, befriended English colonists, saved Smith from death at the hands of the Indians, married settler John Rolfe, and traveled with Rolfe to England to recruit new colonists. She has been lionized in poems, songs, and a hit children's movie of the 1990s. Smith, leader of the Virginia Company colony, recorded thorough descriptions of Indian culture. Down the Colonial Parkway, more than one hundred re-created eighteenth-century gardens (overleaf) are spread over Colonial Williamsburg's 173 acres. Archaeological excavations conducted on many sites revealed the remains of walkways, brick walls, and fence lines, which helped to determine the shape, size, and structure of gardens and outbuildings.

CAPTAIN
JOHN SMITH
GOVERNOR OF
VIRGINIA
1608

Most of Colonial Williamsburg's gardens (right) were planted from the 1930s through the 1950s in the refined Colonial Revival style, reflecting a nostalgic vision of the nation's colonial past. Through "landscape archaeology," the park's nonprofit foundation is gradually reworking its gardens to represent a more historically plausible— and less manicured— setting. The Governor's Palace (opposite) is one of the architectural attractions at Colonial Williamsburg. In 1699, after nearly one hundred years of battling famine, fire, and Indians, the leaders of the Virginia colony abandoned Jamestown for a new capital, named for the reigning King, William of Orange. Thanks to substantial bequests from John D. Rockefeller Jr., the Historic Williamsburg Foundation began preserving— and later restoring— the old colonial capital in the 1920s.

The tranquility of the Town of York, a bustling colonial tobacco port, was shattered in 1781 when American and French forces defeated British troops in the Revolutionary War's decisive battle. At the Yorktown Victory Center's recreated colonial army encampment, costumed characters (above) fire cannons to the delight of most observers. Up the James River, Shirley (right)—Virginia's oldest plantation—was founded six years after settlers arrived in Jamestown. The mansion, whose pineapple roof decoration was the colonial symbol of hospitality, was a supply center for the Continental Army and survived the Peninsula Campaign during the Civil War. Anne Hill Carter, wife of "Light-Horse Harry" Lee and mother of Robert E. Lee, was born there. Shirley Plantation is still a working eight-hundred-acre farm.

Virginia's 1785 state capitol (left) in Richmond, modeled after a Roman temple in Nîmes, France, was the first public building in the New World built in the Classical Revival architectural style. Although it served as the capitol for the Confederacy during the Civil War, the building was not torched by invading Union forces. On April 27, 1870, a crowd squeezed into the Supreme Court of Appeals chamber, collapsing the floor; sixty-two people died. President Jefferson Davis's office (above) contains numerous Confederate icons among the fifteen thousand artifacts, photographs, books, and art objects at Richmond's Museum of the Confederacy in the expanded C.S.A. executive mansion.

Richmond's gloriously restored Carpenter Center for the Performing Arts (above) opened as Loew's movie palace—"an acre of seats . . . in a garden of dreams"—in 1928. The stage in the doughty "Lady of Grace Street," unused for almost fifty years, is now the scene of a myriad of performances. The 1895 Beaux Arts Jefferson Hotel (opposite), built by fabrics merchant and former Confederate major Lewis Ginter, is synonymous with twentieth-century Richmond history. Its original amenities included a Teleseme—a predecessor of the telephone used for room service—and palm trees from South America. The Jefferson closed in the early 1980s before undergoing a massive renovation. Its Palm Court, home to Richmond sculptor Edward Valentine's statue of Thomas Jefferson, is now the registration area. Live alligators once lived in pools beside the statue; today, cast-iron gators have replaced live ones.

A walnut spiral staircase (opposite) held tragic memories for the second owner of Richmond's Bolling Haxall House, now owned by the Woman's Club of Richmond. Physician Francis T. Willis's granddaughter died after a headlong fall down the stairs. The women's club, which could not afford $50 to repair a damaged balustrade during the Great Depression, funded a multistage restoration, begun in 1986 and partially underwritten by the Historic Richmond Foundation. Haxall, the original owner, made his fortune in an ironworks. Another smelter on the James River was the leading producer of cannonballs, bullets, and artillery shells for the Confederacy during the Civil War. To this day, Richmond is reputed to be second only to New Orleans in America in use of decorative cast iron. An office building on North Laurel Street (above) showcases the material.

STONEWALL JACKSON

Richmond notables have lived on Monument Avenue—considered by some "America's most beautiful boulevard"—since city engineer C. P. E. Burgwyn laid it out in 1889. Monuments honor Confederate heroes Robert E. Lee, Stonewall Jackson, J.E.B. Stuart, Matthew Fontaine Maury, and Jefferson Davis. The statue of Jackson (above), shown ramrod-straight in the saddle at the Battle of Bull Run, was designed by F. William Sievers and unveiled in 1919. On another monument (opposite), created by Edward Valentine and unveiled in 1907, Confederate President Davis strikes an oratorical pose. The statue's thirteen Doric columns represent the eleven states that seceded and two (Missouri and Kentucky) that sent delegates to the Confederate Congress but were prevented from departing the Union. Atop a column stands the bronze Vindicatrix, representing the spirit of the South but informally called "Miss Confederacy."

Richmond's Hollywood Cemetery was named for abundant holly trees at its location, high above the James River. The graveyard became a showplace of elaborate mortuary art and the final resting place of prominent citizens and Confederate heroes, including George Pickett and J.E.B. Stuart. President John Tyler and Confederate President Jefferson Davis are interred there. So is James Monroe, the last of the "Virginia Dynasty" of U.S. chief executives. Albert Lybrock designed his distinctive cast-iron memorial (opposite). Incredibly, no mortar was used in the construction of the ninety-foot stone pyramid (left) that honors the eighteen thousand Confederate enlisted men buried at Hollywood. Outside of Richmond in Southside Virginia, the landscape turns quickly rural (overleaf). Hay is rolled to feed animals over the winter.

The slogan of Danville, the principal city in Southside Virginia, is "Pick a Victorian flower." Architecturally, there are plenty to choose from on Millionaires' Row, one of the pre-eminent collections of Victorian and Edwardian architecture in the South. Most of its homes were built for wealthy tobacco merchants and the entrepreneurs who formed the Riverside Cotton Mills—the future Dan River textile company. Among the latter was John Harrell Schoolfield, who had his fellow founder, contractor Thomas B. Fitzgerald, construct a High-Victorian Italianate mansion (above) on Main Street. Down the street, the Queen Anne "Wedding Cake House" (left) was completed as a wedding gift in 1903 for Barnes and Mary Penn. The lavishly decorated mansion is now a bed-and-breakfast inn.

Tobacco was king in Southside Virginia—though today vineyards (opposite) are increasingly important throughout the Commonwealth. Danville warehouses (above) once brimmed with activity. Indeed, Danville was founded as a tobacco inspection center forty years before it was incorporated in 1833, and thrived long after many other communities in the Old Confederacy suffered economic depressions. Bright Leaf tobacco was developed nearby, and the "Danville system" of auctioning entire lots of tobacco was introduced in the city's warehouses. But this neighborhood in the "Last Capital of the Confederacy"—so named because Jefferson Davis, fleeing from Union forces, moved the government there in the final throes of the rebel nation—eventually declined into tawdriness before the city undertook a massive clean-up and revitalization in the 1990s.

The old stone structure (opposite), built in 1798, was the third Quaker meetinghouse built on this site in Lynchburg. Many Quakers, who opposed slavery, left Virginia for northern states. John Lynch, founder of the city, is buried in the Quaker cemetery behind the house. Randolph-Macon Woman's College (top left) was founded in 1890. Washington, D.C., architect William M. Poindexter employed the red brick, white trim, columns, and classical detailing borrowed from Queen Anne-style academic buildings in Great Britain. Robert E. Lee signed the Civil War articles of surrender in the parlor of the McLean House (bottom left) in Appomattox. The University of Virginia's signature landmark, the Rotunda (overleaf), is a half-scale interpretation of the Pantheon in Rome.

The Cabinet, or study (opposite), was the most private sanctum of Thomas Jefferson's home at Monticello (above), near Charlottesville. After spending five years in France, Jefferson completely redesigned his residence, adding the first dome ever seen in Virginia. Atop his study's rotating writing table he employed a "polygraph" copying machine to duplicate letters, of which he wrote more than twenty thousand during his lifetime. Jefferson reported that the polygraph worked by "copying with one pen while you write with the other." Monticello curator Susan R. Stein quotes him as confessing to John Adams: "From sunrise to one or two o'clock, and often from dinner to dark, I am drudging at the writing table. And all this to answer letters into which neither interest nor inclination on my part enters; and often from persons whose names I have never before heard."

Chatham Manor (left) in Fredericksburg was built in 1771 by planter William Fitzhugh, a frequent host of George Washington and Thomas Jefferson. Washington later bought his mother a house on Charles Street in town. James Monroe practiced law down the street. When Union forces captured Fredericksburg during the Civil War, they converted Chatham into a field hospital. Walt Whitman and Clara Barton ministered to the wounded there, and Abraham Lincoln visited twice. Confederate general Stonewall Jackson fought four battles nearby. Although rampant growth has turned Fredericksburg's outskirts into an exurban bedroom community for Washington, D.C., downtown remains a delightful potpourri of historic homes and taverns, and both pricey and kitschy antique shops. This store's sign (above) says it all about its wares.

George Washington's great-grandfather, John Washington, was one of the first settlers in Virginia's "Northern Neck," the area between the Rappahannock and Potomac Rivers.

There, on the banks of the Potomac, John built a modest estate. His grandson Lawrence, George's father, named it "Mount Vernon," after British admiral Edward Vernon, with

whom he had served. George acquired it in 1754 when he was twenty-two, and enlarged the mansion (above), which his father had constructed in 1735. Several original furnishings

are still on display there. The nation's first president was an avid gardener. His plan for the estate called for three gardens, including an upper garden (right), full of vegetables, flowers, and trees.

There were also a kitchen garden and a botanical array in which Washington experimented with seeds and plants not native to Virginia. All three are meticulously maintained to this day.

Alexandria was a thriving Potomac River tobacco port. George Washington—and Robert E. Lee generations later—walked the cobblestone streets and brick sidewalks that Washington had helped lay out. For almost five decades the city was part of the nation's capital, until it was retroceded to Virginia in 1846. Old Town Alexandria (opposite) has retained many eighteenth-century townhouses. Washington and Lee both worshipped at Christ Church (left), built in 1773. Here, Lee was offered command of Virginia forces in the Civil War. In Arlington, once a part of Alexandria, Union forces took control of Lee's estate and, to taunt the Confederates, built a cemetery (overleaf) for Union dead there. More than two hundred thousand military personnel and their dependents are now interred there.

The U.S. Marine Corps War Memorial *(right)* was sculpted by Felix W. de Weldon, based on news photographer Joe Rosenthal's Pulitzer Prize-winning photo of the flag-raising atop Mount Suribachi on the Pacific island of Iwo Jima after the bloody victory over entrenched Japanese forces in 1945. At Arlington National Cemetery, the gravesites of John F. Kennedy and Jacqueline Kennedy Onassis *(opposite)* are attended by an eternal flame. Nearby, a cross marks the grave of the president's brother, Robert. Rosslyn, *(overleaf)* across the Francis Scott Key Bridge from Washington's Georgetown neighborhood, was named for Civil War-era farmer William Henry Ross's "linn," or waterfall-filled stream. From World War II until a building boom in the 1980s, Rosslyn was a seedy neighborhood of pawnshops, bars, and brothels.

Crystal City (above) is a vast residential, office, and underground retail development along old U.S. Route 1 near the old Washington National Airport, which sprawls over landfill in Virginia, across the Potomac River from the federal city. Rather than create vapid stone and glass caverns, Crystal City's developer, the Charles E. Smith Company, spiced the terrain with extensive landscaping and a variety of public art. Dulles International Airport, named for Secretary of State John Foster Dulles, handled only fifty-three thousand passengers when it opened in farmland straddling Fairfax and Loudoun counties in 1962. Today, thirteen million passengers a year take off on its five runways. Architect Eero Saarinen designed the futuristic concourse (left).

Some of Virginia's most lavish homes overlook the Potomac River in communities like McLean, Great Falls, and Leesburg. The gated mansions of diplomats, generals, U.S. senators, and business executives are graced with rock gardens (opposite), manicured lawns, swimming pools, and tennis courts. The Fountain of Faith (above), a monument to everlasting life at Falls Church's National Memorial Park—one of the nation's most beautiful cemeteries—was the creation of Carl Milles, a Swedish sculptor trained at Germany's Bauhaus School. The effect of the bronze forms' placement is of a moving pageant. "Each figure in the fountain I have known when they were alive," Milles wrote. He called the effort "a presentation of people meeting again" in the hereafter. Overleaf: The Great Falls of the Potomac River is one of Virginia's most striking—and treacherous—displays of nature's power.

Three times a week from September through March, after the sounding of the hunting horn, from twenty to one hundred "members of the field" (above) loose their hounds on any fox who happens to be skulking in the fields near The Plains, west of Manassas. This area of Northern Virginia is horse country. At Locust Hill farm near Middleburg (opposite), thoroughbreds are trained, groomed, and stalled. The big Luck Stone Corporation, founded in 1923, has quarries throughout Virginia. This facility—230 feet deep in spots— in Fairfax County near Manassas Battlefield, harvests graystone and an igneous rock called diabase (overleaf). Many quarries first provided ballast for railroads. Luck's operations supply granite for buildings, rock chips for highways, crushed limestone for farmers, and sand for concrete. Its quarries are converted into lakes or other recreation areas.

In Winchester, site of the annual Apple Blossom Parade, the town symbol— a painted cement apple (above), stands on North Braddock Street in Old Town. Farther south in the Shenandoah Valley, wildflowers brighten the New Market Battlefield Park (right). Here in 1864, Confederate troops— including 257 teenage cadets from the Virginia Military Institute, defeated a superior Federal force. At the valley's Luray Caverns, the largest known cave in eastern America (overleaf), crystal-clear underground pools mirror a stalactite formation. In 1905, owner T. C. Northcott built "Limair," the nation's first air-conditioned home, by drilling a shaft into the caverns and drawing cool, purified air into every room.

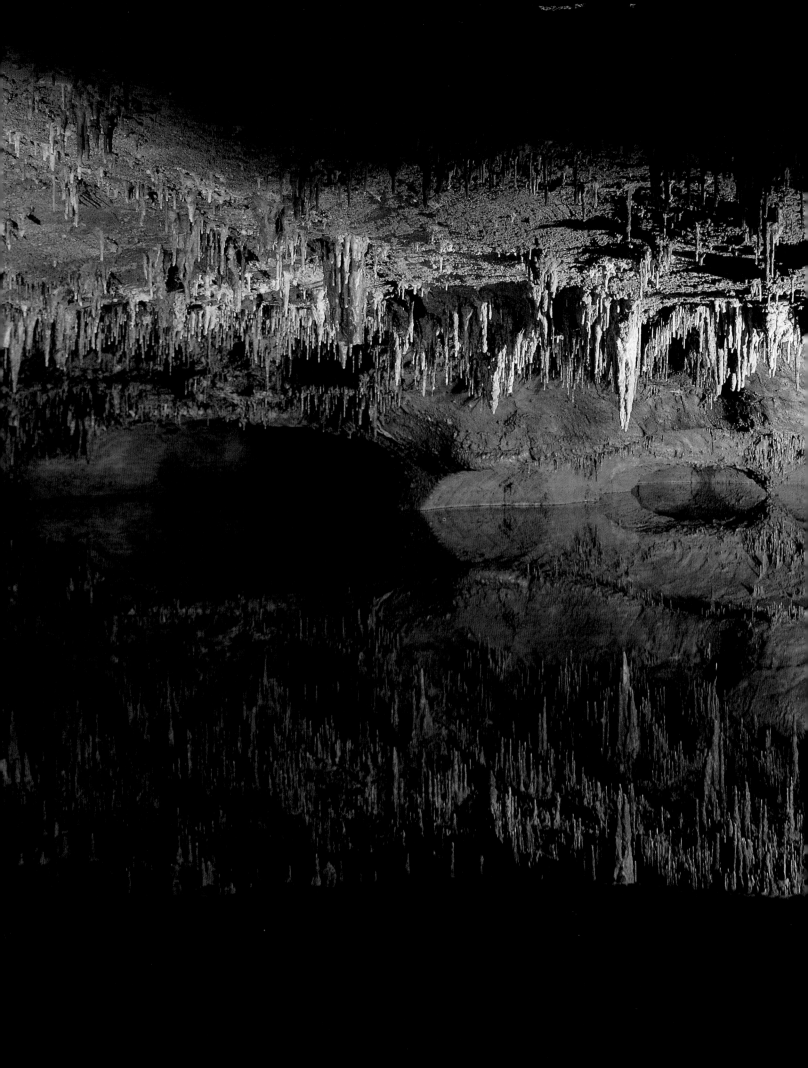

Virginia's historic Shenandoah Valley runs southwest from the Potomac River along two forks of the Shenandoah River, between the Blue Ridge Mountains to the east and the Alleghenies to the west. In 1716, Virginia colonial governor Alexander Spotswood led an expedition to the top of the Blue Ridge, from which his party brought back lavish accounts of the fertile valley below. Soon thereafter, English and Scotch-Irish settlers poured into the area. Because the valley was the "granary of the Confederacy," Union and Rebel armies repeatedly fought to control it. Eventually the Federals virtually laid waste to the region, sending it into a long economic recession. Today's farmers have built modern houses and swimming pools (left), planted charming perennial gardens (above), and sown crops that have prospered (overleaf).

The Museum of American Frontier Culture near Staunton has reconstructed authentic working farms from Europe and Botetourt County, Virginia, to teach about life before immigration and about the lives the immigrants established. Pictured (opposite) is a reassembled 1630 farmhouse from Worcestershire in England's West Midlands. The Buffalo Springs Herb Farm (above) in Raphine, midway between Staunton and Lexington, presents gardens with a variety of themes and offers herbal products and even "herbal luncheons." Woodrow Wilson's Pierce-Arrow (overleaf) is displayed at the president's birthplace in Staunton. Wilson so loved the automobile, built in Buffalo in 1919, that he bought it (for $3,000) for his personal use on the day he rode with his successor, Warren Harding, to Harding's inauguration in 1921. Made of cast aluminum, the three-ton "vestibule suburban car" was powered by a forty-eight-horsepower engine.

Thomas Jonathan Jackson was a professor of military tactics at Virginia Military Institute in Lexington when he resigned from the U.S. Army to fight for secessionist Virginia. He earned the nickname "Stonewall" while resisting a Union attack at the first Battle of Bull Run. The general is buried in Stonewall Jackson Memorial Cemetery (opposite) in Lexington. At VMI today, cadets still march in crisp formation (top left). Edward Valentine carved the recumbent statue of Robert E. Lee (bottom left) at the chapel of Lexington's Washington and Lee University, where Lee spent his final years as president. He is buried in a family crypt on a lower level. Lee often rode his beloved horse, Traveller, into the Shenandoah Valley (overleaf) to meditate.

In 1774, King George III granted the incredible Natural Bridge (opposite) to Thomas Jefferson, who surveyed and mapped the area (as had George Washington before him). In 1803, two years after he was inaugurated president, Jefferson built a cabin at the site and invited the first American visitors. The Cedar Creek branch of the James River, in the Shenandoah Valley, formed the rock bridge as it carved a two-hundred-foot gorge. Nearby on the property, spring-fed waters of another creek tumble over a series of waterfalls (right). Next to the attraction's visitor's center is a wax museum featuring figures from Virginia and U.S. history—including (above) Jefferson and John Adams signing the Declaration of Independence.

Roanoke, the "Capital of the Blue Ridge," was once Big Lick, a key railroad town. It is also called the "Star City of the South" because of the one-hundred-foot neon star (above) erected on Mill Mountain's overlook in 1949. The platform offers a spectacular view of the Roanoke River Valley (right). Once economically depressed, clean, green Roanoke has rebounded in a big way. A walking tour takes visitors to science and art museums, coffee shops, boutiques and antique galleries, and historic fire and train stations. Roanoke is Virginia's most enthusiastic festival city. Everything from valley strawberries and dogwoods to chili recipes from across the state are celebrated annually.

Roanoke's City Market, which has been rated one of America's sixty-three greatest public places, reminds visitors of New Orleans's French Market. Farmers' vegetable and flower stalls (above) at City Market fill the street in front of boutiques, delicatessens, and coffee and wine shops. The Second French Empire-style Evans-Webber House (left) is a landmark in nearby Salem, the first settlement in the Roanoke Valley. Built in 1882 by John Evans for his French bride, the house features thirteen-foot ceilings and brick walls that are thirteen inches thick. The Salem Fair and Exposition—Virginia's second-largest fair—is held in the Salem Civic Center each year in July.

The classic Uneeda
Biscuit sign (top right)
on the Ewald-Clark
Building in downtown
Roanoke was painted
in 1906 but hidden by
a newly constructed
adjacent building in
1917. In 1991, the sign
was discovered and
carefully restored.
In a blue-collar neigh-
borhood near the Mill
Mountain Zoo, a
devoted Elvis Presley
fan has relocated
The King's Memphis
mansion, Graceland
(bottom right), to her
front lawn. A double-
take is needed to
confirm that this is
a lovingly recreated
miniature. The
Norfolk and Western's
coal-fired 4−8−4
Class J streamlined
locomotive, built
in Roanoke in 1950,
is now on display
at the city's Museum
of Transportation.
Eighteen of these
494,000-pound
behemoths operated
in Roanoke daily
for eighteen years.

Virginia's Explore Park (above and right) is just off the Blue Ridge Parkway east of Roanoke. A living history and nature park on thirteen hundred acres of woods, streams, and meadows administered by the Virginia Recreational Facilities Authority, it opened in 1994. The park allows visitors to experience life in a re-created frontier settlement of authentic buildings in the first century of European exploration of the Blue Ridge Mountains. The park depicts the early encounters between European and African-American pioneers and Native American cultures. Visitors climb aboard horse-drawn wagons and pass a one-room country school, a harvest garden, a pigsty, and a cabin in front of which artisans and bluegrass musicians display their skills. Wildflower, blacksmith, gardening, basketmaking, and quilting workshops are offered throughout the year.

The Booker T. Washington National Monument (left and above), southeast of Roanoke, commemorates the life and accomplishments of Booker Taliferro Washington, born a slave on this Burroughs tobacco farm in 1856. Washington left, uneducated and newly freed, at age nine. He returned for a visit in 1908 as a college president and influential statesman. Washington was an internationally recognized educator, author, and spokesman for his race. He recalled his childhood at this modest farm in his autobiography, Up From Slavery. "There was no period of my life that was devoted to play," he once wrote. His critics charged that his conservative approach to racial harmony actually delayed its quest. Mist and fog, haunting to behold but treacherous to traverse, greet many a day in the Shenandoah Valley (overleaf).

The scenic, 469-mile, toll-free Blue Ridge Parkway stretches from Shenandoah National Park in Virginia through western North Carolina to Great Smoky Mountains National Park in Tennessee. At points such as the Metz Run Overlook (above), the road twists and turns along the crest of the southern Appalachians. Near Buffalo Mountain at mile marker 176 on the parkway, east of Pulaski, Mabry Mill (opposite) is an example of the water-powered gristmills once found on nearly every mountain stream. Blacksmith Ed Mabry built the mill in 1910 and operated it into the 1930s. At this working mill today, visitors can watch a miller grind corn into grits, and wheat and buck- wheat into flour, as the waters from the millrace turn the large wooden water wheel. Corn- fields like the one shown (overleaf) supply some of the grain for the mill.

Thousands of bottles
that pharmacist John
Hope washed in his
swimming pool, then
embedded in mortar
in the walls of his
Bottle House in
Hillsville (left),
create an impressive
mosaic. (See page 13
for a historic exterior
view.) Because of the
ready availability of
hardwood ash and
chestnut trees in the
Shenandoah Valley,
pioneers were able to
build thousands of
zig-zag split-rail
fences (above). After
felling, stripping, and
quartering logs with
wooden wedges called
gluts, farmers would
assemble hundreds of
rails and carefully lay
them out in ninety-
degree angles across
their fields. Since
only gravity holds
them up, they placed
the narrowest logs on
rocks to begin the
process, then layered
heavier rails on top.
Overleaf: Sunset
over the Blue Ridge
is awe-inspiring.

Index

*Immediately upon
its unveiling in 1996,
the statue of tennis
great Arthur Ashe
became the most-
photographed attrac-
tion on Richmond's
Monument Avenue.
Ashe, who was once
barred from playing
at the city's Byrd Park
tennis courts, devoted
much of his retire-
ment to promoting
literacy among
African Americans.*